TODAY

Book 4 – The Fivefold Office Series

COLETTE TOACH

www.ami-bookshop.com

Today's Teacher

Book 4 – The Fivefold Office Series

ISBN-10: 162664036X
ISBN-13: 978-1-62664-036-8

5663 Balboa Ave #416,
San Diego,
California 92111,
United States of America

1st Printing July 2017

Published by **Apostolic Movement International, LLC**
E-mail Address: admin@ami-bookshop.com
Web Address: www.ami-bookshop.com

Contents

Chapter 01

The Future Church

Chapter 01 – The Future Church

When we spent some time in Europe, we had a wonderful opportunity to do a little bit of touring. Unfortunately, we did not get to tour as much as I would have liked, but we did have an opportunity to go and see some castles and ruins, which are things that you do not see in other countries like South Africa and the United States.

Now, I was not much into history in school, but when I am walking through a city that I know existed hundreds of years ago and look at these huge stone buildings, my mind wonders about the kind of life those people lived.

I was looking at the construction and thinking about how, hundreds of years down the line, some of these buildings are still standing. Yes, some of them are ruins or a bit messed up, but they are still there.

If I compare it to our building construction today, you have to be amazed at what they accomplished back then. In many places, if we have one little windstorm, we have to mend rooftops.

I wonder what our houses will look like in another hundred years. Will there even be one brick left upon another?

In contrast, at the castle sites, I saw entire city walls, streets, and bridges that had been there for hundreds upon hundreds of years. They were built with some sturdy materials.

The Fortress

One place that we went to had a fortress that was built on top of a hill. They did not have all the equipment that we have today. So, to build this magnificent city, they carried the stones from the bottom, by hand, all the way to the top of the hill.

Even though most of the buildings were broken down, you could still see entire sections of the wall around the entire fortress that still stood defiantly against the elements. I thought, "Wow. What did this place look like back in its prime?"

What did it look like when the walls were all together, the rooms were all connected, and they had lamps and fires burning? The structure must have been really strong because when enemies came, it withstood all the cannon balls and arrows from the wars that this place faced.

A City on a Hill

When I look at the body of Christ today, I see a very similar picture. I see a building, a city on a hill that had tremendous potential. It was built with a solid foundation and walls. However, over time, it has faced its fair share of cannon balls and warfare. It has also faced the system of the world.

Slowly, over time, these attacks started to corrode the walls. That is probably the most corrosive thing to a building. It is not the times of war that tear down so much, but time that wears the building down.

The elements – the wind and rain that come upon the building slowly eat away at the construction, causing it to fall. This is what has happened to the Church today. The Church was not glorious one day and destroyed the next.

What we see in the Church is not the result of something that happened overnight. This is something that has been slowly corroded and destroyed. Now, when we look back, we can say, "I can imagine how glorious the Church must have been back in the Bible days."

When you read the book of Acts and about the things that Paul and Peter taught, you think, "What must it have been like in that day and age, where every believer was on fire? What was it like to see Peter walking along with his shadow healing people?"

"What was it like when the early believers broke bread day to day, and people flooded in because the Church was so alive?"

A Glory Departed

They did not care about being martyred or persecuted. Their fire was so great. What must that have been like? Every now and again, we see a ruin. We see a little revival or something that reminds us of that original glory.

Well, it is now time for the body of Christ to be restored to its glory. It is time that those foundations are built once again, those walls are constructed, and the roof is put on.

This is what God is calling you to do. This is what God is calling the fivefold ministry to do. They are supposed to restore the Church to its glory because Jesus is coming back for a glorious Bride.

He is not coming for a half dead, limping Bride. When was the last time that you went to a wedding, and the groom stood there looking down the aisle at this poor, bedraggled bride that can barely make it to the front?

How glorious is that? No. Your wedding day is the best day of your life as a woman. You look your best. You want your groom's eyes to pop out of his head when he sees you. You want to be something magnificent.

Preparing the Bride

Do you think that our heavenly Bridegroom is any different? He is not returning for a half dead bride that is struggling her way up to the altar. He is not coming for a Laodicean church.

He is coming for a Church that is hot and on fire and ready for her Groom. He is coming for a bride that is in love with Him.

What is the most beautiful thing about your bride when she walks down the aisle, gentlemen?

Yes, it is good that she looks great, but the most wonderful thing is that she is yours. She has given her life to you. I know for a man that this is the most incredible thing. It is what makes men so protective over their wives - because she is his.

If we are like that in the natural, then how much more is our heavenly Bridegroom like that? The one thing that He desires more than anything from us is not our perfection, but our hearts.

What Jesus Wants

Sure, we can prepare ourselves to look the best we can, but the most beautiful thing about us is our dedication and that we say to Him, "I am committing myself to you. I am giving up my freedoms and everything I have to take on what you have, because I am so in love with you."

That is the kind of Bride and Church that the Lord is coming for. It is our job to bring the Church to this place. One of the fivefold ministry that has a vital part to play in this is the teacher.

Teacher, Prophet, and Apostle

Before I get into the signs of today's teacher, we are going to look specifically at the teacher, prophet, and apostle and how these three work together to build and restore the Church.

You see, the evangelist gets everybody fired up, and the pastor is there to keep carrying it on and make sure that the repairs are made. However, who is going to start building this wall up, brick by brick?

It is going to be the teacher, the prophet, and the apostle. They are the ones that are going to take the stones and put the pattern and functionality together.

Once it is together, then the evangelist and pastor can continue. However, we first need to get the building up.

So, to begin, we need to start building a house. In fact, we need to build a city, and that starts with the teacher. Let us look at the illustration of Ezra and Nehemiah.

The Future Church

Jeremiah already prophesied in Jeremiah 29:12 that the children of Israel would come out of their captivity and that the Lord would restore them. If we look at this as a type and a shadow of what the Lord wants to do in His end-times Church, then the picture blows wide open.

I want to look specifically at Ezra and Nehemiah. In these two characters in the Word, you are going to see how God is going to, and is, right now, restoring His end-times Church.

You will see how the Lord is taking those ruins and crumbled buildings and then adding new bricks and mortar. You will see how He is building it up and restoring it, not to its former glory but to a greater glory than it has ever seen!

Time for the Church's Resurrection

This is not going to be a restoration necessarily, but it is going to be a resurrection. You will recall that when Jesus died, He died as a man, but He resurrected as the Son of God. When He resurrected, He was greater than when He walked the earth.

When God brings this restoration to His Church, He is going to bring it up to its former glory, and then He is going to take it to a whole new level because the resurrection is always greater than the birth.

What we see in the New Testament is the birth of the Church. What we are going to establish in this end-times, as a fivefold ministry, is a resurrection of the Church. The resurrection will be greater than the birth.

It will be more glorious and have more power. Jesus walked upon the earth, and He had the ability to heal the sick and raise the dead. However, when He had come down after being glorified, He said, "At my name, every knee will bow, of things in heaven, in earth and under the earth."

He let us know that every tongue now has to confess that He is Lord because He made a show of every principality and authority openly, and He triumphed over them - He even triumphed over death.

The power that He had when He resurrected far surpassed the power that He had when He walked the earth.

A Greater Glory

The Church had a magnificent start in its birth, but there is coming a time when it will be resurrected to a greater glory. Every believer will be walking as Jesus did on the earth. It is our job to bring that to pass.

We live in some exciting times. When I think about this vision, I feel it burn in me so strongly that I fall flat on my face before God and say, "Lord, I am so honored and humbled."

Jesus said to His disciples, "So many have desired to see the days that you are seeing right now." That is exactly how I feel at this day and age. I remember the Lord gave me such a great revelation in the past.

The Lord said to me, "All through the years I have had my servants on their faces interceding and praying. They were never in the visible church, and you never saw their names out there, but men, women, housewives and businessmen all got on their knees before Me."

He said to me that He has never failed to have one of His servants on their face before Him, travailing and releasing what is about to happen in His Church.

The Lord said that, as they prayed, they had a spiritual baton in their hands. They had a baton that has been passed from one generation to the next.

Passing the Baton

Now as the baton comes to our generation, we are going to begin to reap the fruit and see what has been released and decreed through the years.

Even now in the Church, old writings and teachings are being passed around that were released years and years ago. The Church was just not ready for it yet. They had the baton back then, and they passed it onto us.

It is up to us to take it and run with it as best as we can. We are to finish this race with all endurance, and it starts with restoring the Church. It starts with the teacher.

Chapter 02

The Teacher's Function

Chapter 02 – The Teacher's Function

Nehemiah 8:4-7

So Ezra the scribe stood on a platform of wood which they had made for the purpose; and beside him, at his right hand, stood Mattithiah, Shema, Anaiah, Urijah, Hilkiah, and Maaseiah; and at his left hand Pedaiah, Mishael, Malchijah, Hashum, Hashbadana, Zechariah, and Meshullam.
5 And Ezra opened the book in the sight of all the people, for he was standing above all the people; and when he opened it, all the people stood up.
6 And Ezra blessed the Lord, the great God. Then all the people answered, "Amen, Amen!" while lifting up their hands. And they bowed their heads and worshiped the Lord with their faces to the ground.
7 Also Jeshua, Bani, Sherebiah, Jamin, Akkub, Shabbethai, Hodijah, Maaseiah, Kelita, Azariah, Jozabad, Hanan, Pelaiah, and the Levites, helped the people to understand the Law; and the people stood in their place.

Let us look at this picture here. They had built the temple and walls, and now we have Ezra standing up to explain law. He had thousands of people standing in front of him.

In this passage, we see that Ezra did not stand alone in giving this instruction! Look at that long list of names mentioned. It says that they "caused the people to understand the law."

When I look at this, I see the role of the teacher in the Church today.

It is not going to take just one big teacher to build the walls. If you are looking at a restoration of any building, it takes more than one person to put their hand to the plow. You need a couple of builders.

Putting the Teaching Team Together

You need someone that is good with stone, another that is good with cement, another that knows how to mix water, and someone that does the digging. Each one has their place, and it takes a lot of people to build.

Ezra knew that too. Even though Ezra came with the law and the full understanding of what God wanted, he could not get the people to understand it just by standing behind the pulpit.

He needed others to go down amongst the people and cause them to understand.

Why is it so important for the church of God to understand? We have spoken about the importance of the people being on fire and the pastor taking that fire and teaching them to apply it to every aspect of their lives.

However, what is the foundation of that fire? It should be the Word of God. The Word of God is our foundation. It is where the fire comes from and is the source of the power. If you want a bigger fire, how do you make the flames grow?

You add more wood, right? I remember when we decided to burn an old Christmas tree. We took it to the beach and lit it. Have you ever seen a pine tree burn? Wow, it was a huge flame.

The Source of Power

I did not realize how hot and how high those flames would be. That is what we need to do in the body of Christ. It is good to have a fire, but how do we increase it? Once we have the fire, how do we make it hotter?

How do we take the authority and make it stronger? How do we take the anointing and increase it? Do we pray in tongues? Sure, being in the Spirit is important, but what is the source of all of our power? What was the source of Jesus' power?

It was the Word of God. When the Word of God is our foundation, everything changes. If you have already read through or listened to some of our teachings, you know that we deal with templates a lot - our mindsets or the way that we think.

Why? It is because the anointing comes from within our spirits. If we want to get it out, then we need to deal with our mindsets.

Hindrances to the Anointing

It is our mindsets that hinder God! Our poverty and failure mentalities restrict the anointing from flowing outwards.

Is there anything wrong with the anointing deposited within our spirits? No. There is nothing wrong with the anointing. It is pure, good, fresh water. However, the problem is in our soul - the blockages in our mind, emotions, and will.

You do not need any more anointing. You have it on tap. You are already so full. The Word speaks about us being anointed once. You do not need to be anointed again and again. The anointing is already there. (I teach more on this in my book entitled, *Prophetic Anointing,* so I will not labor the point here.)

The problem does not lie with the anointing. The problem lies in getting it out. This is where the Word of God comes in.

How the Word Removes Blockages

When you start feeding the Word of God in, it begins to change the way that you think.

Consider this. If you are, at any time, involved with a group of a certain kind of people, you will start to think like those people. If you are around geeky computer types, or a bunch of people from any kind of industry, do you notice that they think the same way?

They have the same way of seeing problems. They think the same, talk the same, and have the same slang. Why is that? It is because all the teaching and studying that they have done has formed the way that they think.

Computer geeks around the world sound the same. Sometimes, they even act the same way. Get a bunch of English teachers together, and you will notice that they are the same, universally.

Why is that? It is because everything that they have fed into their minds has shaped the way that they think. They have learned to think in a certain way to the point where they cannot think outside of that pattern anymore.

Now, if you have been called to be a teacher, then I guarantee that the Lord has been challenging you on your foundation and the veils that you have. He has been challenging you on the way that you think. This is because the pattern that you have in your mind right now is blocking the Spirit of God within.

If you want to flow in a greater authority and anointing, then you are going to have to change your mindset. That means that you need to start pushing something into your mind that has the power to transform you.

What does the Word of God say? It says that we will be renewed by the rhema word of God.

> ***Romans 12:2*** *Do not conform to the pattern of this world, but be transformed by the renewing of your mind. Then you will be able to test and approve what God's will is-- his good, pleasing and perfect will. (NIV)*

It is the Word of God that will change the way that you think. It is going to change your mindset.

Now, this is where it gets exciting. When the things in your mind start lining up with the things that are in your spirit, it is like putting two pipes together that fit perfectly.

Fixing Your Pipes

We had an experience with our house in Mexico where two plumbing pipes did not fit well together. Instead of doing a decent job, the builders did what I probably would have... they duct-taped them together to force a fit. Unfortunately, when we turned on the tap - there was water everywhere.

Suddenly, we had leaks in the house, and my husband had to run around fixing them.

He had to go to a hardware store to find the right size pipe so that the water did not flow all over my kitchen again and ruin the cupboards!

How often are our spirits in this same condition?

We have all this water trying to gush out from our spirits, and before it can get poured out where it is meant to go... you discover a leak. You feel the power so strongly from within. But, when it comes out, it barely dribbles out.

You think, "Lord, I felt like such a lion inside, and it came out like a squeaky little mouse. What happened to the rest?"

It is because your mind and spirit are not lining up right. You have not been renewed and transformed in your mind.

The Teacher: Mr. Fix-it

That is why we need teachers. However, how many believers go around saying to themselves, "I am going to get up early and get into the Word of God! It is so exciting. I am going to read and read and read."

Not many that I know do that, unless they are those theological teaching types that do not read the Word but study it. They always press to study the Word, but they never actually learn the Word.

They can tell you a lot about the Scriptures and give you chapter and verse, detailed by doctrine. Unfortunately, they, more than likely, have a greater bondage that hinders the anointing more than anyone else. It is because all they have learned is theology instead of living knowledge.

They need the living and breathing word of God! This is where the teacher comes in. Remember how I said that it is for the evangelist to come and remind the Church of what they have lost and get them on fire? Well, it is for the teacher to make them hungry for the Word.

1. Teacher Stirs up Hunger

Speak to me about the Word for five minutes. I will get you so on fire that you will want to go home and read. Why? Simply because I love the Word. The Scriptures say that the Word came, the Word was with God, and the Word was God. (John 1:1)

The Word is God, and it is living. It has the answer to every need. Therefore, if I need more anointing or authority, then I need some of the living Word inside. The Word says that we do not have the Word living inside of us because we do not believe the one that He has sent. (John 5:38)

This indicates that the Word should be living inside of us. It is a living scripture, and there is no limit to the power you can move in or people that you can reach. There is no limit to the miracles that you can see taking place - because the Word is the beginning of all power.

Of course, you need to add the Spirit, and we will get onto the role of the prophet soon enough. However, if you do not have the Word, then you will not have a good foundation.

Once you have a solid footing in the Word, then you are mature and will not be swept away by every wind of doctrine.

Good Teaching Makes it Taste So Good!

One morning, I went into the kitchen and put some big, juicy chickens into the oven. As I was getting ready for the day, the smell wafting through the house carried me back to countless Sunday dinner meals shared with my family over the years.

Before long, the food was ready, and I opened the oven to find two perfectly browned chickens ready to be served. I peeked into the rice steamer and was met with a waft of nutty goodness from the brown rice.

I hurried to whip up the mashed potatoes until it was light and fluffy. From there, I drizzled some garlic butter over steamed corn. I tossed my green beans with some feta cheese, finishing it off with just enough freshly ground black pepper to give a little bite.

After writing that... I am hungry! I do not know about you, but I want to head to the kitchen and get cooking!

You see, that is what the teacher does with the Word of God. He has a way of painting it so that it makes you hungry and wanting to read the Word.

2. Teacher Breaks the Word Down

When the Church comes to the place of wanting to get into the Word, then the teacher comes and feeds them.

I make the food, make you hungry while you smell it, and then I sit you down at the table and feed you.

That, in its essence, is the function of the teacher. A teacher has a way of making things simple and breaking them down. They have a way of reminding us that there are solutions that we can find in the Word.

When you are not a teacher, you know that answers to everyday problems are in the Word, but have you ever tried searching for them when you have a problem? It is not so easy.

Your eldest daughter is being rebellious – where do you find a scripture to solve that problem? How do you find out how to deal with hormonal swings in the Scriptures?

Well, a teacher has a way of taking the Word and applying it as a sword to you in such a way that you sit there thinking, "Wow, I never saw that in the Word before."

I have come to realize that the greatest conviction I can give when I am training someone is with the Word of God. It is not what I think that matters.

3. Teacher Uses the Double-Edged Sword

That is why the symbol for the teacher is a sword. It is a double-edged sword that cuts and divides. I do not just take any scripture and throw it at you. You must take the Word of God and apply it practically to peoples' lives.

It is easy enough to tell people what is right and wrong. Anyone can look at someone sinning and see where they are failing. How many times have you tried to point these things out, without any effect?

Now, if you pick up the Word, under the inspiration of the anointing, and speak the Word of God, then it will come out as a double-edged sword and convict. This makes all the difference in the world.

They can kick and scream and like or dislike you as much as they want - but they cannot fight the Word. Our authority is vested in the Word, and it brings stability – a stability we sorely need in the Church today.

4. Teacher Flows in Word and Spirit

Why do we see so many doctrines going astray? Why do we see so many people going off in the wrong direction? It is because they are going solely by the Spirit. They are just going off on all their revelations, but their revelations are not confirming the Word.

Revelations should confirm the Word. Also, if I throw one hundred scriptures into a teaching, does that make my revelation accurate? That does not cut it either.

You cannot say, "I got a revelation. Let me see how I can back it up with Scripture."

No. When I get revelation by the Spirit, the Word and Spirit come out simultaneously. They flow together.

One word comes after the other. I do not need to say, "Turn with me to this and that scripture," because the Word is living inside of me.

I might be sharing scripture, but it flows out of me just like a prophetic word. However, instead of a prophetic word, the Word of God comes out. It should be such a simple flow.

The teacher has the ability to do that. Keep in mind though that all teachers are not the same. You have different teaching types, and this will more than likely put a lot of things into place for you.

5. The Teacher Trains Using the Word

Perhaps, you are more prophetic, and now God is leading you to teach. When you know what each of these types look like, then you will be able to put yourself in that place.

Let me tell you something. Regardless of what your ministry is, you need to know the Word of God. The

Word needs to be living inside of you. It should be that way for every believer.

I am not talking about head knowledge here. I am talking about being trained.

> ***2 Timothy 3:16*** *All Scripture is given by inspiration of God, and is profitable for doctrine, for reproof, for correction, for instruction in righteousness,*
> *17 that the man of God may be complete, thoroughly equipped for every good work.*

I love the end part of verse 16.

I love this word "training" because we need our minds to be trained and conditioned, so that we can come to maturity and be fully equipped. Yet, before we can be fully equipped, we need to be trained.

If you are an athlete, you do not just jump on the field and start running. It takes some conditioning. Your body has to go through its paces. You have to work up your stamina and change your diet.

You have to condition yourself, and then you can run the race with all endurance. Sometimes, our problems can disappear simply with some training.

If I am not strong physically and cannot run the race because of this, but then I get myself fit, that problem or weakness disappears. Most times, people are in bad situations, and it looks like an impossible problem. But, all they need is to know the Word.

Working Out Weaknesses

Most times, there is not a weakness or flaw that someone needs to deal with, but it is simply that they are ignorant of what the Word of God says.

If they knew what the Word of God said, then their problem would disappear because they would know what the right thing is to do.

We need to start training the body of Christ in the Word, but it starts with making them hungry. Then, when they are hungry, they are ready to get into the Word, and ready to receive what you have to give them. Then, we can start filling their heads with the good stuff.

What are we competing against here in the world? We are competing against the radio, TV, the Internet and other such media. Even when you go to a restaurant, the TV is playing. It is horrible. The world's doctrine is coming at you all the time.

Combatting the Spirit of the World Together

What is happening to the Church through the process of constantly hearing these things? Your mind is being trained with the spirit of the world. This is what we are up against right now. If we are going to take those building blocks and build up the Church, we are going to have to come with a message that is louder.

That is why we need the evangelist that comes in and says, "Switch that TV off. Let us start focusing on the things of God." Then, we need the pastor to come and say, "I have an alternative for you. Let us go and have a barbeque, play a game, or do something else."

Then, the teacher comes in and says, "While I have you all here, let me retrain you." Each fulfills an incredible function. We need to change the way people think. We have to let them know that what they learned is wrong.

It means repetition, repetition, and more repetition. By the time you finish this book, you are not going to remember every last lesson, but you will remember the pictures and words that I shared over and over again.

The Effect of Repetitive Teaching

One day, you are going to stand up and open your mouth, and then guess what is going to come out? Whatever you were taught will come out. You will do it without even thinking. Sometimes, you do not even remember where the teaching came from.

That is why patterns from the past are so difficult to deal with, and that is why God has been challenging you. It is not as if you have these old patterns from the past that you cling to on purpose. It is just that you do not realize that you have them.

However, you must realize that whether you agreed with the teaching you heard or not, it has conditioned your mind if you sat under it for a long time and heard it again and again. If you heard it, saw it, and felt it, then it conditioned your mind.

Whether you like it or not, you will walk in the pattern that was put into you. How many people say, "I will never be a mother like my mother was?" Yet, what happens when you have your own kids?

Time for Re-Programming

You shock yourself by finding words tumbling out your mouth that cause you to say, "Lord, I repent because I sounded just like my mother!" Did you want to? No. You hated hearing it growing up. Did you mean to? No. It just came out. Why? It is because that is the way you were programmed.

When I am challenging you about doctrines, and you say, "I do not believe that, and I never agreed with that pastor or teaching." It does not matter, because you sat under that teaching long enough for a pattern to be established in your mind.

I do not care whether you liked it, agreed to it or not. If you sat under it long enough, then it changed the way you thought, and it conditioned you. That is why the job of the teacher is such a long one and also why it is one of the longer ministry trainings too.

Your job as a teacher involves a lot of repetition because you are "training for righteousness." Only then will the people of God mature. I know that it sounds like a lot of work, but the reward remains.

The most exciting part about being a teacher is that, if you do your job right, the foundation you lay will remain. It will be like those castles I spoke about at the beginning. Years down the line, people will still be able to see the work you did.

Prophetic words come and go, but a strong foundation remains. It often feels like a thankless job. It can get frustrating to have to repeat yourself so many times, but I promise - it is worth it.

When you have invested all you have, and done all you can to train God's people, there is no greater reward than knowing that the work you have done will remain for years to come.

CHAPTER 03

TEACHER TYPES

Chapter 03 – Teacher Types

That is why we also need different teaching types. When it comes to training people, you cannot train them all the same way. Everyone is different.

You have to reach people from different angles. You will have different temperaments, different upbringings, different cultures, and different archetypes. You cannot train a Swiss like you train an American because their cultures are so different.

If you approach a Swiss the same way you approach an American, they will not receive from you. In the body of Christ, it is the same. We need different kinds of teachers to reach different kinds of people.

The Pastor Teacher

Therefore, the first teaching type we have is the pastor-teacher. Pastor-teachers are the guys that took Ezra's word that I read about in Nehemiah and went and made the people understand it.

Imagine the teacher as the guy who prepares this big meal. Imagine this big roast that sits over a fire for hours. When it is done, you do not just go and start chomping on that huge piece of meat.

You come with your plate. Someone will cut the meat, and you will get your portion. That is the job of the pastor-teacher. The teacher will prepare the meal.

Then, the pastor-teacher will break it up and serve it in bit size portions that you can understand.

Ezra stood up there with the whole book of the law. Yet, it took those other guys to take that and cause the people to comprehend it. Ezra had the whole picture, but the people did not.

He needed the pastor-teachers to come and hand out a piece at a time until they could understand the whole thing. That is the job of the pastor-teacher. His teaching is extremely practical, and he has a great way of being able to break things down.

Local Church Function

He loves bible studies. In the local church, he is the one that can just look at a scripture and make it so simple to understand. We need these guys because when it comes to the Word of God, from Genesis to Revelation, it is like being faced with this huge roast.

Where do you begin nibbling? Which part is the best to begin with? The pastor-teacher has an ability to look and see which part is the best and what will suit you just right. He has such an anointing to break it down and make getting into the Word so much fun and so simple.

That is why I love our bible studies because they are not just about the teacher just standing up and teaching, but also about asking everyone what they think about the Scriptures. It is about seeing what everyone else sees in the Scriptures.

The pastor-teacher draws the people to be involved, and to understand a piece at a time. As I share this, I am sure that you are already starting to see the local church come to life.

We already have them fired up, and they are sitting comfortably in their seats. Then, we say, "Guys, you are at the party, and now it is time to eat." The pastor-teacher can break up the Word and ask the people what the Lord has been sharing with them over the week.

The people can say, "The Lord gave me this scripture, and it meant this or that. The pastor-teacher is the most obvious teacher that we see in the Church. It is one of the first that you learn to function in.

Also, another great thing about the pastor-teacher is that he does not originate. The guys that went out to cause the people to understand did not originate the teaching. Ezra did. The pastor-teacher just takes what the teaching apostle lays down, and they teach it to the people.

The Prophetic Teacher

Now, let us look at the prophetic-teacher next. When you look in Acts 15, you will see that Silas and some others go to strengthen the brethren in Jerusalem with many words. If you stand up to teach as a prophet, you will teach under inspiration.

This was probably the greatest function of my ministry in the beginning. Why? It was because if I was going to be able to teach prophets, then I needed to be a prophetic-teacher. That means you must be inspiring and speak by revelation.

Inspirational Preacher

The interesting thing about the prophetic-teacher is that all his words apply for "the here and now". They are rhema words for today. This is not the kind of teaching, necessarily, that you would take home and listen to again and again.

That is because it is a teaching that is applied to your life right now. It is not always a foundation that you can build on. Sometimes, it is, but mostly when I am preaching in this way, I go to the Lord and ask Him, "What do you want me to share with your people today?"

Then, He will say, "My people are battling with finances, and you need to motivate them in this area." He might say, "My people are discouraged, so I need you to encourage them." Sometimes, He may even say, "There is sin in the camp, so you need to bring conviction."

When you go to the Lord, and He gives you revelation like that, then it means that He wants you to preach prophetically. If that is the case, then you are not going to want a lot of sermon notes. At max, you should have two to three scriptures written down.

In fact, three is even overkill because scriptures will come to you as you speak because prophetic-teaching is where you "chase the rabbit" all over the place. This is because, as you are preaching and teaching, the people's hearts are crying out to the Lord, and the Lord is going to tell you what they need.

I experience this so often. I will be saying one thing, and then the Lord leads me into another direction. Then, as I am sharing that thing, the Lord leads me in yet another direction.

These are the times that when the message is over, people come to you and say, "As you were preaching, I was asking the Lord a question, and you gave the answer." Then, I think, "Aha. It is your fault. You were the reason that the Lord led me all over the place."

It is fun. Prophetic-teaching is really stress-free because you do not know what you are going to say. It is like giving a really long prophetic word.

You know how us prophets love to carry on. We love the sound of our own voice!

Keeping the Balance

The only word of caution is that when the rabbit gets off the track, it is enough. Know when the anointing has left, and it is time to sit down. Please do not go for another hour. That is why I said to keep the notes to a bare minimum.

If I have lots of notes when I preach in this way, I can go on for hours.

When a teacher teaches, his notes are structured and clear, and he does stick to them. For prophetic-teaching, I want to give you a heads up.

Make your notes just in case something happens and the anointing leaves because someone breaks the flow. That way you do not stand in the front looking dumbfounded with no words to share. You want to look good.

Keep your notes there, but I guarantee that at the end you will say, “What were in my notes again?” You will not even look at them. If that happens, chill out. You were just functioning as a prophetic-teacher.

That teaching is applying something to the hearts of the people right now. At a later stage, if someone has the exact same problem, and they listen to the message you preached, it may inspire them again.

However, it is generally the kind of Sunday preach where you are ministering to a specific need in God’s people, and it is for now. It is like fresh bread that is relevant for now.

There are lots of teachings like that on our ministry videos website too. After hearing the messages, you go away remembering how it made you feel more than remembering the principles in the actual teaching.

Everyone Has a Place

You remember the picture and the message that the Lord had for you, but you do not remember everything. If that is the case, then you are under a prophetic-teacher and fulfilling a vital role in the Church.

I do not have a three-course meal three times a day. Could you imagine what I would look like? You do not always need to feed people the whole horse all the time. Yet, some people are like that. If you get them going, they just want to give you the whole lamb.

Sometimes, you just need a snack. If you are anything like me, there is nothing like a good chocolate mousse with some whipped cream and sprinkles on top and also a side of strawberries. Dessert is so good.

That is what you look forward to all the time. You skip through the big stuff, so that you can make it to dessert. We need it. That is the stuff that makes life fun. We need the prophetic-teacher because they are the dessert.

They are the ones that make you feel good, and we need it. We need a combination of good, solid doctrine and some fun stuff. What is a party without some dancing, singing, and joy?

It is good to have the Word and make them hungry for a good, solid meal. Yet, once they are satisfied and know the doctrine and the Word, then you need to fluff it up a little. You need to make the Word fun and exciting.

You need to motivate, encourage, and fire them up. Just say, "Lord, give me what you need for your people." Then, stand up as a jug, and let the water pour in. Just be that open vessel, stand there, and let the water come in and then spray out of you until every need in the place is met.

You will hop here and there, and at the end, you will not even understand why you gave your message the title that you gave it because it has nothing to do with what you taught. However, you go with the flow anyway because it feels so good.

Then, the flow will stop, and you know that it is over. It is like a prophetic word. If you have prophesied, then you know that the word will come and come and then eventually stop.

Do not make the mistake of pushing beyond what the Lord intends because then you may get into deception, and people may start falling asleep. That is some personal experience talking there.

If You are a Prophetic Teacher

If you tend to flow in this kind of teaching more often, then you should journal all of your messages, and ask the Lord how He wants you to reach the people before you get on your hobby horse.

In fact, I journal all my messages anyways, even if they are not prophetic-teaching messages. You need to know if He wants you to feed them a whole lamb, if you need to break things down a little more, or if you should serve a snack platter.

From there, He will say something to you that will let you know the way that you need to teach. Sometimes, the Lord may tell you that there is an element missing in the people's understanding concerning the flow of the Holy Spirit.

Then, you know that you need to flow as a pastor-teacher. You will be taking the bigger teaching and breaking it down for them. You will be giving them good, solid teaching. You will be laying it out plainly for them.

If you have a teaching function, do not be surprised if the Lord switches you between them. Be open to whatever the Lord has. Yet, you will find that, from season to season, the Lord will emphasize one or the other.

Like I said, at the beginning of my ministry, I was the fiery prophetic type. So, a lot of my teaching was prophetic. As I matured in the Lord, He pushed me into the teaching ministry. I say, "pushed", because I went kicking and screaming. I am ashamed to say that.

However, I love the teaching ministry now. Yet, at that time, the prophet in me wanted to burst out. I just wanted dessert all the time. As you go into teaching, it is going to change, and you will probably be there for a season.

Just be open to where God wants you right now. If you have been very comfortable flowing in one, then perhaps a time will come when the Lord will start moving you over to another.

What I love about the gifts of the Spirit is that it is not about your gifts or anointing, but it is about what the people need. Maybe they need some good, solid teaching? Possibly, they just need to be motivated with the Word of God?

It is not for you to say. That is why I said that you need to journal before teaching.

The Apostolic Teacher

Now, let us take a look at the apostolic-teacher. A couple examples of an apostolic-teacher are Ezra and Moses.

They are the ones that lay down the doctrine. They got the whole lamb or roast all put together. They have the full picture, which is what I am giving you right now. I am explaining to you where each of the fivefold fits in the local and universal church.

You cannot sit a new believer down and say, "Read this book." Please do not do that because he will choke. Rather take a piece at a time and reteach it. Do the "pastor-teacher thing" first.

There are those that may be mature enough to eat the whole lamb, and that is great. Let them read the book. However, a new convert is not going to get it. You will have to give them a piece at a time.

Start with inviting them over to your house. Say, "Let us have some time together in the Lord." Then, reteach to them, in your own words, what you have received and understood.

Give them the doctrine a bit at a time, until they eventually understand the whole doctrine. Then, if you give them my teachings afterwards, they will say, "This Colette woman stole everything from my pastor."

That is the kind of teacher that Apostle Paul was. He said in 2 Timothy 1:11,

> *To which I was appointed a preacher, an apostle, and a teacher of the Gentiles.*

Paul laid down what we call foundational teaching. That is the teaching that I am doing now along with what I taught on the *Prophetic Field Guide Series*.

Anybody that has been in our prophetic training knows that you do not take the whole prophetic school and give it to a new convert.

This is one of the reasons why the Lord lead me to write, *Practical Prophetic Ministry*. It is for those that are still easing into the prophetic.

My book, *Practical Prophetic Ministry,* is pastor-teacher teaching. I took all the principles from the *Prophetic Field Guide Series,* and I pulled out bite size pieces so that people could get a full overview, in a simple way, without needing to go through all seven books!

Are you starting to see the difference between the teacher types?

Ezra

Ezra gave the whole book of the law, which is a lot for someone to comprehend all in one day. That is why he needed the others to go out and feed it to the people. Ezra shows us the role of the apostolic-teacher. He gets the full revelation.

Yet, not every apostle is called to that. Some will be like David. Some will be more prophetic. Not every apostle will be the same. Do not put the pressure on every apostle to be a teacher like this, because Peter was not one like this.

However, Peter was the Lord's right hand man. He wrote Peter 1 and 2 and did go and teach, but he was more of a prophet in his delivery. What a perfect mix Peter and Paul were.

I just love the Lord's sense of humor. The Lord sends Peter, who is more prophetic, to the Jews, which are the ones who had all the law. Then, he sends Paul, who had all the law, to the Gentiles, who did not have the law.

Paul was actually more qualified to teach the Jews than Peter was because he grew up as a Pharisee. He was the man's man. If there was anyone who could fight using the law as a weapon, it was Paul.

Paul

Yet, the Lord has Paul take all his great knowledge and throw it into the trashcan. Then, Paul comes to a whole new doctrine that says, "I have come to the conclusion that we are justified by faith without the deeds of the law. So, let us move on." (Gal 3:11, Rom 3:28)

He said, "All these things I consider lost compared to the excellency of the knowledge of Christ." (Phil 3:8)

Here comes Peter with something that the Jews never had. He came with the evangelistic power of God.

He was just as much of an apostle as Paul was. He just displayed it more in the power of God rather than in teaching. I am laying down the teaching types clearly so that you can see the full picture and know where God has you right now.

Also, learn to identify it in others. A couple said to me once, "Why reinvent the wheel? You already have the teaching, so why do we need to reinvent the wheel?" You are right. You do not need to reinvent the wheel. All you need to do is take pieces of it and hand it out as God gives it to you.

Take the apostles teachings and reteach them a piece at a time. That is why apostles tend to teach at a higher level - so that we can give the pastor-teachers the apostles' doctrine, and then you can take it and feed it to the people.

Passing it on in the Local Church

When you do that, do you know what is going to happen? Their minds are going to change, and the spirit that is inside of them is going to start bubbling up. So, what is the function of the teacher in the local church?

He is the one that makes the word alive. He makes believers so hungry for the word that before the next meeting, they are getting into the Scriptures because the first thing the pastor-teacher is going to say is, "What did the Lord show you in the Word over the past week?"

They are going to be so excited to share what the Lord showed them in the Word. Each one is going to start blurting out what God showed them because it is so exciting when you get revelation.

If you can hear God through a journal, it is great. However, there is something unique about getting revelation from the Word. It is amazing when you open up the Word and a scripture speaks directly to you. It is so powerful.

The Power of the Word

It is like a seed gets planted in you that no one can take away. That scripture becomes part of your foundation. You will preach on that scripture for years to come. Yet, revelations in journals come and go, and they are for the moment.

Yet, when you get a revelation from the Word, it is like a brick on that broken down wall of a building. It puts a brick into place for you. If we could start putting bricks into place for every single believer, then the Church will start rising up.

However, it starts in the local church. That is where you have your home church leaders. The elder must be apt to teach. He needs to be a pastor-teacher. He needs to be a jack-of-all-trades. He needs to be able to take the Word and break it down for people.

Every local church should be on fire, have answers to their problems, and have knowledge of the Word. When you look at that, you will see that there is such a variety of meetings that you can have.

You should be having them all. Why stick to the same type of meeting every week? Go get *How to Start a Home Church*. I give you some ideas in there. Let all of the fivefold ministry have an opportunity to minister to God's people.

Let the people not know what to expect at the next meeting. Let them wonder what God is going to feed them today.

On a practical level, after reading a book such as this, you will go back to your home church and reteach it to them a piece at a time. You will say, "Guys, I have some new revelation. I have some apostles' doctrine for you."

You can have your own seminar stretched out over a few weeks, so that you can reteach it. The sky is the limit. That is the role of the pastor-teacher in the local Church.

Then, in the universal Church, it is clear to see what the role of the teacher is there. He is there to be a part of laying down the doctrine. Also, this is where you should be having Bible college, because we need to train the minds of the teachers.

Teaching the Teachers

The teachers should be teaching the teachers and instructing them in doctrine, gifts of the spirit, and all the things that others could not care less about learning. You can teach them, train them, and then send them out to get the rest of the body of Christ excited about it.

This is also where the public meetings take place. That is how Ezra did it. He had all the people there, and he stood on the pulpit and shared. I love that picture. He stands there and gives the whole doctrine, and then the remaining teachers go and cause the people to understand it.

That is the best thing. You stand up and have a public meeting and a good teacher to give them some good, solid meat. Then, you go back to your local church, and the pastor-teacher there says, "Ok. Let me break down in more detail now what you heard."

Isn't this the pattern that Paul followed? He went from place to place, church to church, and taught the doctrine. Then, he left, and it was up to the elders to cause the people to understand, and to have them continue on in the apostles' doctrine.

The Apostolic Teaching Pattern

So, let me challenge you with a question. What is the pattern of your apostle? If you are an apostle, then what is the pattern that God has given to you? Do you have a clear picture of the apostle's doctrine, that it is not just their doctrine but yours as well?

Is it so clear that it is not just something that you heard, but something that belongs to you? I am asking this because you cannot give out something that does not belong to you.

It is not good enough for people to just listen to what you teach. The people who listen have to live what you teach because when they live what you teach, then they will have the Word of God living inside of them.

Then, when He speaks, they will recognize His voice because His Word is living inside of them.

When I teach you something, it should not reach just as far as your mind. This teaching should go into your heart, your spirit, and then into your life until eventually you start thinking that you got the revelation yourself.

That is how it should be. Teachers teach and teach, and then someone says, "Wow, I got this revelation, and I want to share it with you." Then, you think, "I have only been teaching it for the last seven years, but I am glad that you got it."

They think it is their revelation, even though they heard it from you over and over. Good. That is the purpose of the teacher. What is your apostle's doctrine? If you are an apostle, what is your doctrine? What is the pattern that the Lord has given you to lay out?

Then, what is left to do, guys? Now, we must put our hands to the plow, pick up a trowel, get ourselves some stones, and start restoring God's end-times Church!

CHAPTER 04

WHAT TEACHERS DO

Chapter 04 – What Teachers Do

> ***Matthew 13:52*** *Then He said to them, "Therefore every scribe instructed concerning the kingdom of heaven is like a householder who brings out of his treasure things new and old."*

Everyone remembers the day that they first fell in love. How old were you when you fell in love for the first time? Perhaps, it was with the spouse that you have today, but that is highly unlikely.

I am just being honest. I am sure that your spouse understands because the truth is that around fourteen or fifteen, you started realizing what love was or, at least, what you thought love was.

We never forget the first time that we fall in love. It makes such an impact on us. In many ways, it conditions us for who we look for in the future. It is such an engaging time and season in our lives that we never forget it.

It is just like when you have your first child or your wedding day. These are moments that are like beacons along the road of your life. They are times and shifts that take place and give you a point of decision where you need to go left or right.

Well, I remember the first time that I fell in love with the Word. Up until that time, I had been the pastor, and most definitely been the prophet. The Lord even used me a bit in teaching ministry.

The Character of the Word

I had preached *The Way of Dreams and Visions,* and I had also done some apostolic teaching. I taught some principles, gave out the knowledge, and preached.

However, in 2009, when my husband and I took over the ministry, the Lord said to me,

"You think you know Me, but I want to tell you something about Me. My character is diverse. Even after fifteen years of marriage to your husband, Craig, you are still finding out things about each other. How much more with Me?

You think you know Me because of your relationship with the Holy Spirit. You think you know Me because you have come into My throne room. You think you know Me because you have experienced the gentle breeze of Jesus.

However, there is an entire dimension of My character that you do not know, and that character is to be found in the Word."

An Epic Journey Into Scripture

So, He took Me on a journey. I would daresay that He wooed me into the Word, and I started to fall in love. From that moment, I started to see a character of the Lord that I had never seen of Him.

I saw a side of Him, His nature, through eyes I had never seen with before. For the first time, I came to realize something so profound. I realized that the Word was alive.

I grew up knowing this in principle and had read the Scripture about how the Word is living, powerful, and sharper than any two-edged sword - A scripture I often enjoyed to quote.

However, it is one thing to know it and another thing to experience it. I would pick up my Bible, and instead of journaling or having the Lord speak to me through that inner voice, His voice was found in the pages of the Word.

The Word was talking to me, and I realized that the Word was more than the law. The Word was a person, and He had a nature, a character, and a nuance. There was poetry to it.

The way that the Lord said things in the Word, hinted to His sense of humor, deep jealousy, brewing anger, and even hostility at times - there were all of these nuances found in the Word that made His character come to life.

That Special Spice

Think about someone that you love. What is it that you love about them? Is it just that they are nice to you? No, it takes a lot more than that. It is all the nuances and the things that make them so different that make you fall in love with them. That "special spice" that gives them a flavor that no one else has.

The fact that they have weaknesses that make you laugh is why you love them. The fact that they are clumsy and quirky or laugh at the silliest things makes you love them.

It is these parts of our character that make us endearing to one another. It is this part of God's character that we miss so much because we do not see the Word as living and powerful.

By the time you are done reading this chapter, you are going to want to rush to the Scriptures to get to know the Lord because you will see more of His temperament in the Word than you ever will when you are in the Spirit.

You experience more of His temperament through the pages of Leviticus than you can imagine, when you look for it and know how to find it.

The Teacher: Expressing the Nature of the Word

Each of the fivefold ministry expresses the Lord in a different way. The prophets will express to you the nature of Jesus. They will express His grace, love, nurturing, and acceptance that only Jesus can bring.

The apostle will express to you the nature of the Father. He will express His authority, righteousness, and direction for your life. He will express that this is to be taken seriously, and there is no messing around.

The evangelist expresses to you the nature of the Holy Spirit. He expresses the fire, glory, and conviction.

However, the teacher expresses the nature of the Word. That, in essence, is what the teaching anointing is all about.

And just in case you thought I forgot about him, if you have read *Identifying Today's Pastor,* you would have read how the pastor does a little bit of them all.

The First Teacher: Moses

Moses was definitely the first teacher in Scripture. Since there has been a law, there have been teachers. There is always someone there to explain to us the deeper things of God.

If someone who is a prophet picks up the Bible and goes through it, I promise that they will likely miss some of the things that I have expressed to you in this chapter so far.

Now, the teachers will be saying, "I saw that. I knew that." Yet, the prophets are likely saying, "Really? Wow! That is true. I should have seen that." However, you did not see it because you are a prophet.

You are viewing ministry through the eyes of Jesus. You are viewing the world and the Word through different eyes. As a prophet or evangelist, you are viewing the parts of the Word that fit your view.

Evangelist? You are going to see the conviction. You are going to see the Hell, fire, and damnation. You are going to see Jesus or see His grace. It depends on what eyes you are looking with.

When a teacher looks at the Word, he steps back and sees the broader picture. He sees it all. He understands and has a wisdom that only God can give. That is why he is able to take the law, and all the bits and pieces, and feed it to you in a way that you say, "I should have known that. Duh! That is obvious. If I read the Scripture, that is exactly what it says."

However, you did not notice until the teacher came along and pointed it out to you. You read the same scripture one hundred times, and then the teacher comes and explains that law to you. The light bulb comes on.

You think, "That is what God meant."

When the teacher teaches, you do not just understand the Scripture, but it is as if you take on a piece of God. You understand the Lord and His nature a little bit more.

You are drawn more to Jesus, the Holy Spirit, and to the Father. You feel equipped, like you received something that built you up. That is what the teacher does and is meant to do.

The Need for Genesis and Exodus

You see, we have Moses who went up and down the mountain, as we have already discussed, getting the law.

We have the Ten Commandments, Numbers, Leviticus, rules and regulations, but I think to myself, "How horrific would it be to read all of that if we did not have Genesis and Exodus?"

The Lord knew that we needed Genesis and Exodus so that we could choke down Leviticus. Yes, we need the rules and regulations and the "thou shalt" and "thou shalt not", but it is boring to everyone else... except to the teacher!

The teacher has a way of taking the "thou shalt" and "thou shalt not", and all those crazy rules and regulations, and teaching on them in a way that you say, "I never saw that before. That is actually very interesting."

They have a way of taking Numbers that says, "This person begot this person who begot this person who begot this person," and sharing it in an interesting way.

If you are not a teacher and just read the Word for fun, all you think is, "Lord, can this book just end?"

Now me, I love reading that stuff. I am weird like that. I see so much more. I think,

"Oh! So, this person was married to this person. This means that Rahab, the harlot, did not only get saved from death, but she married one of the leaders.

I wonder how that was for her? She saved the nation of Israel, and in so doing, lost everyone in Jericho. She married someone in leadership. Man, that guy must have paid a price."

You will be amazed what you can get from that book. That is what the teacher does. He looks at the bigger picture. He does not just look at "this person begot this person, who begot this person".

The Teacher Brings Color!

The teacher steps back, looks at the timeline, and sees how it all fits together. That is why we need teachers. They can step back and say, "I know that Job is a bit of a hard book to understand. Let me help you out with that."

"Let me take you back to Genesis and the beginning of Exodus so that you can understand Leviticus. This way you can understand the purification rights and why the tabernacle and the priests' office had to be exactly like the Father said."

I teach like this all the time, especially when I teach on the pastor, or on the apostle, because it is in the first five books of the Bible that you are going to find the rules and all the answers that you are looking for regarding them.

There is more there than you realize, but it takes the teacher to bring that out. It makes it exciting. The teacher brings color. He takes the black and white, the "thou shalt" and "thou shalt not", and he colors it in and gives it a signature.

The next thing you know, what was so boring and dry becomes very exciting.

Lives the Word

> ***John 5:38*** *But you do not have His word abiding in you, because whom He sent, Him you do not believe.*

> ***John 1:1*** *In the beginning was the Word, and the Word was with God, and the Word was God.*

I have met people who have read the Bible cover to cover and still do not know it. They studied and went to Bible college and got a degree in Theology. They studied every nuance, every Hebrew and Greek word, and I look at them and say, "You still do not know the Word."

> **It takes a lot more than reading the Scriptures to know the Word. The secret is in the fact that the Word is living.**

> **You have to live the Word, not know the Word.**

That is what separates the sheep from the goats. The teacher does not know the Word. The teacher lives the

Word. When there is someone who lives the Word, they have a way of expounding it in such a way that even Leviticus is interesting.

Chapter 05

The Price the Teacher Pays

Chapter 05 – The Price the Teacher Pays

Scripture was not written in a day. Let's take a look at our scripture again.

> ***Matthew 13:52*** *Then He said to them, "Therefore every scribe instructed concerning the kingdom of heaven is like a householder who brings out of his treasure things new and old."*

This is why teacher training is one of the longest out of the five. It is because an accumulation takes place. You do not get the revelation in a day. Moses did not get the revelation in a day.

In fact, Genesis was written thousands of years after the fact. It took time. Moses did not just say, "Alright. Let's just write today and get Numbers, Leviticus, and Exodus done."

No, it took time. It takes time to become a teacher. It takes time to accumulate. Then, as you live it, read the Word and study it, the pieces will suddenly start to fall into place.

How long does it take me to prepare a message? It takes me five to ten years. Do you think I lived this in a day?

Do you think I am teaching this by saying, "Let's go into the Scriptures, the Strong's Concordance, and let's reference it? Perfect. Now, I know exactly what a teacher is."

This is absolutely not what a teacher does. A teacher does not just skip through the Word, pull out great revelations, and say, "Here you go!"

Every single believer has the indwelling of the Holy Spirit. Every believer can find revelation in the Word. That does not set a teacher apart. What sets a teacher apart is that he lives that revelation one step at a time, one piece at a time.

He does it until he comes to the end of his journey, pieces all those revelations together, and then presents to you the full picture. That is how a teacher ministers, and that is why it takes so long, and why we do not see enough of them in the Church.

Who wants to go through all of that travail? Who wants to be like Moses and spend forty years in the desert and another forty years here and there? It took time for him to put this together.

He was way up there in years by the time he wrote Genesis. He had already gone through it and had those times face to face with the Father. This is how it is with the teacher.

The Corporate Anointing of the Word

Now for me, I looked at the travail, and that deterred me from the teaching ministry.

My dad is a fantastic teacher. I thought, "I am an expressive. I do not want to take that long to learn a lesson. I just want to get in the spirit and release the anointing and power and get going."

I came to realize that when you love the Word and live the Word like this, each puzzle piece contains a piece of anointing and authority as well. By the time you have put all those pieces together, it is like a corporate anointing starts taking place.

As you stand up and present the word, the people begin to live it. Perhaps, you have noticed that a little. If you have gone through our prophetic training, you begin to live the teaching.

Why? It is because I lived it, and I preached to you what I lived. That is the power of the teacher. It is not about being intelligent, or about having a revelation in the Word.

That is not good enough. Just seeing the Word and being able to explain the Word to you is not good enough. That does not define a teacher. It may be someone who is in teaching ministry, but it is certainly not someone who is standing in the office of a teacher.

Someone who stands in that office has lived that revelation again and again from every possible case scenario. Then, when they stand behind the pulpit, they take all the experience of life, the revelation from the Word, the anointing from the spirit, and they pour it out.

It comes at you like a force, a hurricane. It is a sneaky hurricane though because it is teaching. It is not like the evangelistic fire that you feel and shout "Glory!"

There is none of that happening when a teacher is teaching. However, wait until you go home. The teacher plants seeds as he teaches. It is a sneaky anointing.

It gets into those cracks, just as you open your heart saying, "Yeah, that makes sense."

Right in that moment, when you let down your guard and let that word, that seed into your heart that the sower was throwing out, you received that anointing.

When a seed is sown and goes into the ground, you do not really notice at first.

Those Sneaky Seeds!

We travailed over our little grass patch in our backyard at our ministry center in California.

We threw seeds down, over and over again, trying to get some grass, until the entire ground was covered with seeds.

One day, I went out, and I could not see the seeds anymore. I thought, "Did the birds get the seeds? Where did all those seeds go?"

Of course, they had gone into the ground. However, it was such a subtle thing. I did not get woken up in the middle of the night, sensing that a seed just went into the ground.

In fact, I kind of blinked, and it was gone. That is the teaching anointing. It is sneaky. There is no big boom or hurricane. It plants something in your spirit. When it plants it in your spirit, it begins to grow.

When you leave from the presence of the teacher, things start to happen. Circumstances start to lead you in a certain direction. Revelation starts to flow that you did not get before.

You start to see things that you did not see before. The more that you nurture that seed, that principle that you received from the teacher, the more it affects your life. That is why the teacher is one that certainly lays a doctrinal foundation.

However, it is not done overnight, just like that grass did not grow overnight. Trust me, there was travailing, watering, and maintaining until it grew.

Sometimes it feels like a thankless job, does it not? You are teaching and teaching, sowing seeds, and then the birds come and eat the seeds. Then, you make the mistake of throwing seeds on hard ground.

You may also sow seeds on a patch of grass that has so many weeds that it gets choked up. Yet, as a teacher, when you sow that seed in a heart that is ready, you can get up to a thousand-fold return on the seed that you sow.

Ready… Aim… Throw That Seed!

That is what we aim for. You see, I throw out a lot of seeds to a lot of people all the time, and then I watch to see where my hundred-fold return comes from.

I look around thinking, "Which one of you is it going to be? Surely, one of you is going to reap a hundred-fold return, a thousand-fold return, but not everyone will."

I remember going through this struggle. You invest so much, and this goes for anyone in ministry. You give and pour out and say, "Lord, I am doing so much. Am I wasting my time? It seems like nobody is listening."

You come to a point where you think, "I am just going to give up throwing these seeds on the ground. This grass is never going to grow."

The sun comes down and scorches it. One little seed starts to grow, and then it is gone.

We finally got a patch of grass that was just big enough for me to sit on. Then, I came back out the next day, and the gophers had eaten it. Do you feel my pain?

That is how it feels to be a teacher sometimes. You think, "Oh my goodness! They finally got it. Never mind… it's gone now."

You say, "Thank you, Lord. They got the revelation."

"Oh no, I spoke too soon. There goes the gopher. It took that little blade of grass that was finally manifesting some fruit."

However, you keep sowing and sowing. You will see that you will not only get a hundred-fold, but up to a thousand-fold return. That is why we do it. The one that reaches the thousand-fold return is the one that goes out there and changes the Church.

We are going to change the Church one person at a time.

> **It only takes one key player to influence a whole nation. We just need to reach that one key player or be that one key player.**

We need to keep doing what God has called us to do. Sometimes, as a teacher, you feel like you are travailing for nothing. You feel like that sower, sowing the Word, and the gophers, birds, and sun are getting to it.

However, there is one time that you are going to sow it on a field that is going to reap fruit. Let me tell you, when you see those rise up that you have sowed into and see them prospering and flourishing, that travail will be worth it.

The Teacher – One who LIVES the Word

The Word is not something a teacher reads. It is not even something that a teacher knows. The Word is something that a teacher lives. His life is a testimony of that. His life is the doctrine.

I have spoken to many theologians. They know their doctrine, but they are so boring. You would think that I would enjoy heavy theological doctrine, but it bores me to death.

I do not want to see someone teach the doctrine. I want to see them live it. I want to see it in their life.

If you believe that God heals, I want to see it. If you do not believe that God heals, I want to see that as well. I do not care what your doctrinal persuasion is - I want to see it in your life.

Do not stand behind the pulpit and tell me what you believe and think, because I am looking at your life as a model and saying, "Teacher, if that is what you believe, do not tell me - show me. Then, I will believe your message."

What are people going to follow? Will they follow a word or a model? If you want to be a good teacher, then live the Word of God, and then others will live the Word of God.

Then, they will pick up the Scriptures one day and say, "Aha... that is what I have been living."

The Word will then be living, powerful, and sharper than any two-edged sword. That is how the teacher makes the Word come alive. He does not just make it sound good.

Even someone in the world can preach a good message. They can be charismatic and entertaining, but can they make you live it? Can they make it something that you do not just understand, but something that you become?

It is a powerful anointing, and it brings a separation between the way that the world views a teacher and the way that God views a teacher.

In the world, you see someone at a blackboard, and they tell you what they know. They say, "One plus one equals two." That is what most people define as a teacher.

No, that is not a teacher. It is not about understanding. It is all about wisdom. That is why it is a process and why it takes so long.

Nothing Comes Easy

The teacher is one that has travailed for the truth. I have had some words with God about this.

When I was a prophet, it seemed so much easier. I would say, "Lord, I need this anointing." Instantly, it was right there.

I would say, "Lord, this person needs a miracle from you." The revelation would come right away.

Being a prophet was so effortless. You just get in the spirit, and God tells you what to say. You can just be the donkey and blurt it out. It is easy, and I miss those days.

Then, He took me through this teaching calling, and I said, “Lord, give me the word.”

After waiting a few seconds, tapping my hands on the table, I said, “Any minute now.”

He said to me, “Knock, and the door will be opened. Seek, and you will find. Ask, and you will receive an answer.”

I said, “Lord, that sounds like work.”

So, I knocked. Then, when I did not get an answer right away, I said, “Nobody is home,” and I walked away.

He said, “No, you keep knocking, and you keep seeking.”

He started to bring me spiritual kids that I did not have answers for. I said, “Lord, give me revelation.”

“Go to my Word.”

“Give me revelation.”

“Go to my Word.”

“Give me… ok… I will go to the Word.”

I studied and suffered long. I sought Him. Between what He told me in my journals, what I lived, and what I read in the Word, slowly, I started to get the answer. However, God never handed it to me on a silver platter.

He made me work and pay a price for it, as if I was pregnant with a baby and had to nurture it, carry it, and go through the pains of labor before I could birth it. That is what it was like for every single principle that I teach.

I did not just get it overnight.

"How did you get all this revelation?"

"I just had a dream, and it was there."

I wish! It is not like that for a teacher. They travail. They say, "Lord, I have a problem with the flesh, with anger, with bitterness, with lust, with hurts from the past."

Pregnant With Principles

For me, I had a tremendous problem with fear and guilt. They crippled me to the point that sometimes I could not even stand behind the pulpit. The fear of failure and guilt stopped me.

It was not even real guilt. It was just me worrying about letting God down so much, to the point where I could not even stand up to minister.

I said, “Lord, there is something wrong with me. Would you just fix it?”

He did not answer. So then, I would journal about it.

Now, have you ever had one of those journals when you go to the Lord with something that is really on your heart, and He talks about the weather?

You say, “No, Lord, I really need to deal with this problem.”

He just talks about something else completely.

You say, “Lord, you are making me work for this.”

He says, “Seek, ask, and knock.”

I sought Him, I cried out, I travailed, I got mad, I shouted at Him, I begged Him, I studied the Word, and I begged Him some more. Then, He gave me my answer.

He whom the Son sets free is free indeed. He set me free, but I had to do everything wrong first before doing everything right. Then, He gave me the revelation.

Why all of this travail? I had to go through this process so that I would understand your struggles, and so that I would not preach from knowledge, but from compassion and understanding.

When I am helping someone to break free of fear or guilt, I want to give them my heart. I want to give them my life. I do not want to just give them a principle that is going to bounce off the wall.

I do not want them to just say, “That was a nice piece of information.” I do not want them to have “nice” from me. I want them to have the reality of the Word from me.

I want them to know that it is available to them and that they can break free, because I broke free.

I want to say, “I know it is a struggle. I know that it is hard, but I know that God can and will set you free. Now, let me show you how.”

As we walk along the road, I can say, “Do not fall into that pothole. Do not sit there - it is a bush of thorns.”

I can only teach that because I went down that road and fell into those very potholes, and sat on those very thorns.

It is a travail. Revelation does not come easy to the teacher. Sometimes, they get jealous of the prophet.

“You guys just get visions. Things just pop out for you.”

This is not the case for the teacher. The Lord makes them work for it. It is a process, but that is where they receive the anointing. That is the cool part.

With the prophet, the anointing comes, you speak, and then you are the same sinful, lousy vessel that you were when you started. The evangelist even more so.

The Lord has used the most sinful men to be evangelists. You say, "Lord, how can you use them?"

As a teacher, you can wake me up at four o'clock in the morning, and you will get the same anointing as when the Holy Spirit is present in a meeting.

I made a joke amongst our family. We have a personal twitter account amongst our close inner circle. I saw how some of the team was putting up a bed and watching me preach online in their pajamas.

I said, "I wish I could preach in my jammies. That looks so comfy."

One of my spiritual sons said, "Mom, I have seen you preach in your jammies. It is still just as anointed."

They come and knock on the door and sit on the edge of Craig's and my bed late at night, and out comes the Word. You can wake me up anytime, and it is still there. That is what I love about being a teacher.

Always Added To

When you collect these principles and gain these things along the way, you never lose them. In fact, it is like building a building. You add to it.

As a prophet, sometimes you think, "Lord, did I miss you?" He gives you a revelation here and there, and many times those revelations seem so disconnected.

It is not the same for the teacher. It is a very clear track, progress by progress, step by step, and it adds things, both old and new. Then, when they come to teach, they are able to put together the full picture for you.

So, if God is making you beg, and has always made you beg and never just allowed things to land in your lap, you are in a good place. With every revelation that He gives you, He has given you a piece of anointing, and it is an anointing that remains.

Yes, it feels like a seed, but a seed is no less powerful whether it is in the packet or in the ground. It is still a seed, even if it feels like nothing to you. It is something that will remain, and it will bear fruit in people's lives from generation to generation.

What has changed the course of history more than anything? Doctrine.

For the Pentecostals, was it just the outpouring of the Spirit that changed the Church, or the doctrine behind it?

The fact that God can heal and that the Holy Spirit is available to every believer - that doctrine allowed the Holy Spirit to manifest.

When the people believed, the signs followed, right? If people do not believe, signs are not going to follow. It is for the teacher to plant those seeds that bear forth fruit and give people faith.

When they have faith, the glory will come. It was only when the children of Israel cried out that Moses could be sent to them.

It takes time for people to develop faith, and that is why it is such a painstaking job that we have as teachers to continue teaching the same things again and again, until it takes root.

Chapter 06

The Teaching Anointing

Chapter 06 – The Teaching Anointing

It is because the teacher goes through such a continual learning process that the anointing he carries remains. It bears fruit long after he is done teaching. How do you know if you have sat under an anointed teacher? You continue to live that message long after he has taught it!

If you have a little bit of confusion after reading or listening to many messages from a teacher, relax. You just picked up all those seeds, and you are living everything you read.

If you are under a teacher, learning all about the fivefold ministry, by the end of it you may not know if you are an evangelist, a pastor, a teacher, a prophet, or an apostle! Do not worry. It will settle. You are just living the anointing. It will all come into balance.

The pendulum will stop swinging, and you will find your zone and be happy again with who God has made you to be.

Just know that when you sit under an anointed teacher, you will live it. Even now, when you think on your experiences of the past, think about someone that you sat under and immediately started living what they taught.

You were sitting under somebody in teaching office. They impart to you their life, not just the Word, because their life is the Word. They give you a foundation.

A Sneaky Sharp Sword

Let me tell you something about the teacher. He brings conviction. That sword is sharp. I have stood up and given prophetic words for many years to many people.

However, when I learned to pick up the sword of the Word, I found that it is sharp and that it cuts. Nobody can argue the Word. People can duck a prophetic word.

They can even duck the anointing. They will jump out of the way of that waterfall and say, "Oh no, that word was for you, brother."

There is something tricky though about trying to duck a sword that is coming at your head. You cannot duck a sword when it is pointed straight at your heart, aiming directly at you.

You cannot duck the Word of God when you know very well that it is you that God is talking to. Then, you have the teacher in your face saying, "You need to deal with the flesh."

They are using the Word with the anointing, and there is no ducking. I can see that every message.

I can always tell when the sword was allocated for a specific person. The person flinches or something, and I know that they just picked up a seed.

As a teacher, you can see where that particular sword cuts and hits the heart. Since it is the Word, it is indisputable.

You cannot say, “That was not for me.”

The Word of God says, “Unless you love your brother, you hate God.”

“Well, that is...”

“No, this is not my idea or me trying to get on your case. The Word of God says this. Now, do you love the Lord?”

“Yes.”

“You are a Christian, right?”

“Yes.”

“So, you believe the Word?”

“Yes.”

“Well, that is what the Word says.”

We do not always like what the Word says, but we all know that it applies to all of us. So, if I have to love my neighbor, so do you because the Word says so.

I can stand up and wax prophetic on you, and you can say, "That was just your idea. That was the enemy, and it was deception. You were just pushing your agenda."

However, when I stand up and quote scripture at you, there is no ducking that. That is why it is so awesome to be a teacher, and that is why they will deliver the most conviction, especially from the pulpit. It is a conviction that remains.

I have sat under many ministries and operated in many ministries. For the evangelistic and the prophetic, the message you receive is really in the moment.

You are cut to the heart and weep before the Lord, and it is so good. When a teacher brings conviction though, like I said, it plants a seed, and that conviction continues. It's sneaky! You might not even recognize that you got hit at first.

You leave that place, and that Word goes in your head. The next thing you know, you are dreaming about it. Everywhere you look, you are seeing it. The Lord gives you a spear in the side here and a spear in the side there.

You say, "Ok, Lord, I get it. I give up."

The Word continues to work itself in you. That is the anointing that the teacher has. It does not just come and go, but it is an anointing that remains.

Supernatural Wisdom

Also, when someone flows in the teaching anointing, they have a supernatural wisdom. They see things in the Word that nobody else has.

It is one thing to love the Word. I think many believers love the Word just as much as I do. However, it is another thing to be able to express it. That takes a teacher with a bit of wisdom.

When you are under a teacher, you say, "Of course. I see now. That is obvious."

They have the ability to bring that out.

They give you the meat from what they live. They take the laws, Leviticus and Numbers, and they lead you into a revelation of Christ.

Functions of the Teacher

> ***2 Timothy 3:16*** *All Scripture is given by inspiration of God, and is profitable for doctrine, for reproof, for correction, for instruction in righteousness,*
> *17 that the man of God may be complete, thoroughly equipped for every good work.*

This is the go to for the teacher. This is his function in the Church completely. Ever since there has been law, there have been teachers to express that law.

In the Old Testament, Moses got the law, and he expressed it through Genesis, Exodus, Leviticus, Numbers, and Deuteronomy.

The prophets came along, and they expounded on that law. Then, John the Baptist came along, and He transitioned us to a new law. Then, Jesus came and said, "I have a new covenant that I am giving to you."

Paul and the rest of the apostles picked up from there and birthed a new generation. They gave us some new laws. They said, "It is not good enough to love your neighbor as yourself. From now on, you love as I have loved you."

Jesus said, "Here is a new covenant that I give to you. Love one another as I have loved you."

It took people like James and Paul to take this new law and explain it to us in a way that we would understand it.

They gave it to us, piece by piece, about loving our neighbor, putting aside the old man and putting on the new man. They explained, piece by piece, all of the laws since Genesis.

Paul referred to the Old Testament again and again. He said, "Do you not see what God was saying? We need to put off the old and put on the new.

The whole purpose for the sacrifice and the altar was so that Jesus would be the final sacrifice and that through Him we would have salvation through faith. We do not have to go to the high priest. We can now go to Christ."

He had to explain and color it in and make it all make sense. As you read through the Old Testament, knowing the New Testament, you will see Paul all over the place.

He took those nuggets that were black and white and he made them come to life.

> **As long as there is a law, there is going to be a teacher to explain that law to us.**

However, it is going to take a lot more than head knowledge. Even the scripture that I just shared with you says that all Scripture is God breathed. Those that wrote the law, even in the Old Testament, the Holy Spirit had to come upon them.

They did not write from their heads. Although, they did not have the indwelling of the Holy Spirit, the Holy Spirit would descend on them so that they could write.

The hand of God had to be on them, and it is no different today. You cannot stand up and preach without the hand of God on you. It has to be something that you have lived, not just something that you understand.

With that, you will release the anointing.

CHAPTER 07

SIGNS OF THE TEACHING CALLING

Chapter 07 – Signs of the Teaching Calling

Now, I am going to move onto the fun part. I have eleven signs to explain the function of the teacher in office. These are the signs for those that are meant to take the law of God and expound on it for us.

1. Makes the Word Come Alive

The teacher makes the Word of God come alive. You want to read it and see the parts where God has a sense of humor. You want to see the parts where He is angry. You want to see His character.

You think, "What are you seeing in the Word? Where did you see that? Show me that. I have never seen that in the Word before. Where did you get that story and illustration from?"

After the meetings are over, you are going through the Word, trying to find out where he got that from. They make you want to read the Word because they love the Word so much, and how can you not love the Word too?

When I talk about marriage and how much I believe in it, and I get all doe-eyed and romantic and excited about it, every single woman wants to get married.

You cannot help it. When you love something, it is contagious. Since the teacher loves the Word so much, it is contagious, and you begin to love the Word just as much.

2. Causes You to Live the Word

He also causes you to live the Word. He sows spiritual seeds in your heart. After you are finished reading this book, you are going to live it.

You may even be one that gobbles up many seeds at a time. You are like a chipmunk with puffed out cheeks because you are taking in all the seeds that you can.

When you do this, you will find that you are living many things at once, and you will not know whether you should evangelize, prophesy, or teach. You just take it all in.

3. Most Lessons are Learned Through Failure

Most of the lessons that a teacher has lived and teaches on are lessons of failure. He always messes up first before getting it right. You mess it up not once or twice, but to the point of embarrassment and beyond, before you get it right.

Then, one day, the penny drops, and you think, "Aha! I should deal with my rebellion."

That is how a teacher learns lessons, through failing. This way, he is able to relate to others.

When Paul teaches, you can see that this is a man who has lived what he teaches. You read through the book of Romans, and you say, "I understand you."

"Although those things are lawful for me, they are not expedient. Who knew?"

"Although I can do anything, there are probably some things that I should not do."

"I have this thorn in my flesh, and I cried out to God again and again, but all He said was, "My grace is sufficient for you."

I hated it when God told me that. I thought, "Lord, just take the thorn away."

He said, "My grace is sufficient. Work it girl. I am not handing it to you. Work for it."

I messed it up badly first. I tried the prophetic thing, the evangelistic. I pulled out all my spiritual gifts and principles, and nothing worked. I messed up every last one of them and applied the wrong principle at the wrong time, and I was still stuck.

Then, the Lord said, "Good. Once you are finished wrestling with yourself, maybe you will realize that my grace is sufficient for you. You need me in this process, not your principles. Die to your principles."

Every lesson that the teacher preaches and has learned has begun with failure.

4. No Answer Ever "Handed on a Platter"

No answer was ever handed to the teacher on a platter. Not only does he go through failure and tough times in life, but no answer was ever handed to him.

If there is one thing that I realize for teachers in their preparation and training phases, it is that, as a teacher, you are going to experience more problems in life than any of the other fivefold.

Why is this? It is because the Church needs solutions to those problems. So, you are going to have marital problems, sexual problems, bitterness problems, anger problems, lust problems, son and daughter problems, even parental problems.

You are also going to have problems with your pastor, your boss, your finances, and your health. So, do you want to be a teacher? It is so much fun.

Why the travail? It is because whatever the Church needs, you need to give them the principles they need. You cannot just give them a scripted answer, "Thus saith the Lord, He shall set you free."

"How? Why? Where? When? Please tell me these things."

The Lord says, "Whatever you do, it is going to prosper."

"Ok. What should I do? How should I do it? That is a great prophetic word. I feel pumped and engaged. I am excited to go out there and… do something. What should I be doing?"

That is where the teacher comes in because the answer was never handed to him on a platter.

A prophet will come in and say, "God is going to restore your marriage."

You are so excited, and you go home and tell your spouse, "God is going to restore our marriage."

Then, you sit there waiting.

"Any minute now, it is going to just come right."

It takes a teacher to explain how it is going to come right.

He will say, "Have you thought of being nice? Husbands, when was the last time you bought your wife flowers? Wives, when was the last time you gave your poor husband sex?"

That is what the teacher does. He gets in there.

Why can I say things like that? I can say it because I lived it. I failed one hundred times, and I can say, "This is what you do not do, and this is what you do. This is what works, and this is what does not work. Most importantly, all of this is based on the Word of God."

They give you a doctrine to live by in your home, your family, and your workplace. A teacher can have mandates in a variety of places. You will see that teachers can even zero in on a specific realm where they really become proficient.

Some will focus on families, some on marriages, and some on business. You will especially see this business mandate coming more in these end times in the fivefold ministry.

That is a whole different point. However, the point is that a teacher will experience a variety of problems. As you rise up, God will have you zero in on a specific realm, just like Peter was to the Jews and Paul to the Gentiles.

Their messages had a very specific environment. For me, I teach on the fivefold ministry and on spiritual parenting. However, the Lord uses me in a lot of different ways.

I had a lot of problems and failures. I did it wrong first, and this is why I can teach you to avoid those potholes. That is why no answer is ever handed on a platter to a teacher.

5. Lays a Foundation That Remains

The teacher lays a foundation that remains. It is a seed that grows in you. Being a spiritual parent, I teach my spiritual kids both natural and spiritual things.

As my daughters got old enough, I took them into the kitchen and taught them how to cook. For my spiritual daughters, I taught them how to put on make-up and how to be good wives.

I did not teach them major doctrinal stuff. However, it is funny how those things change the course of a person's life, and it is a doctrine that remains.

I can go to the ministry center in South Africa right now, and it would be like being in my own kitchen. The food tastes the same, and the way that they arrange it is the same.

I did not have to tell them to do it that way. They also minister the same way. Why is this? It is because it is a doctrine that remains. When you teach with that anointing, it sticks.

What you do not realize is that when you receive from a teacher, whether good or bad, fortunately (or unfortunately) it sticks. It is a seed that is planted when you open your heart.

Hopefully, it is good seeds that you received. It has the power to create a foundation in you. That is why, in prophetic training and especially teacher training, God will begin stripping those wrong doctrines from you.

You see, you do not even know the doctrines that you believe. You do not even realize what is behind what you are saying.

We will say, "Do you know that you believe in this doctrine?"

"No I don't."

"Oh yes you do. You say this, this, and this."

"Yeah. So what?"

"Don't you realize that this is that doctrine?"

"No, I do not believe in that doctrine."

"Well, somebody that you were under did, and you received that doctrine into your heart. You believe it, even though God has given you a different revelation."

It is crazy. When you have sat under a real teacher, you receive that doctrinal foundation, and you do not even question it. You just think, "That is in the Word, right?"

I had an interesting challenge. Perhaps, the prophets will relate to this one. In our school, I get to view the reports that students send to their lecturers. I always keep my eye on them to see the progress of each student.

So, one student submitted this project and reported how she had ministered to someone and said, "I just felt that I needed to tell them that they needed to learn to love themselves and to forgive themselves."

Denise said, "Ok, you believe in that?"

"Yes! I really do."

"Alright. I want you to do a study in the Word, and I want you to pull up every scripture that tells us that we need to forgive ourselves. Then, please give me the list."

If we could forgive ourselves, what would we need the blood of Christ for? We are not forgivers. God is the forgiver. He is the one that cleanses us from all unrighteousness. How can you cleanse yourself?

The student in question took up the challenge, convinced she was right, only to return dumbfounded, "I really thought it was in the Word. I have heard it from the pulpit for years, but right now, I cannot find any good scriptural foundation for it!"

When you sit under that doctrine long enough, hearing it from the pulpit, the TV, and the social workers, it is going to stick.

Do yourself a favor and try to find the scripture in the Word that says, "Thou shalt love thyself" or "Thou shalt forgive thyself". Am I challenging your doctrine?

I hope so because that is not in the Word. Yet, when you sit under a teacher, you do not even realize it. You just think that this is your own conviction. You say, "That is my conviction. It is what I believe."

Then, you start going through the Scriptures, and you realize that there is not one single scripture in the Word that says that. The teacher lays a foundation that remains.

It is a tremendous responsibility. Do not think that you can stand up and preach just anything that comes to your head. Before I stand behind the pulpit, I travail. I am nervous, and my hands are shaking.

My husband says, “Lovey, you have been doing this for years. What are you nervous about?”

I say, “Don’t you understand the responsibility? If I teach something wrong, and they think it is cool and the latest trend and take hold of it and run with it, they are taking that tare into the fields of the kingdom of God.”

I cannot take that seed back once it has been sown. It will lay a foundation. If you come to just one of our seminars, no matter how many seeds you take, it is going to influence your life, even if it is only one seed.

So, I better make sure that the seeds that I am sowing are good seeds and that there are not any tares mixed in with the wheat.

That is why we have to go through as teachers. We must go through the fire, and through those experiences, so that, by the time we come to pouring out what we are living, it is pure and clean and not contaminated with the world.

It cannot be contaminated with psychology, great ideas, intellect, or theology. It has to be the pure, beautiful, living Word of God.

6. Convicts and Instructs

The teacher also convicts and instructs. I think that stands for itself. Do you think that I did not notice that the sword hit you? I know that it hit you. It is sharp.

It cuts to the heart, and it makes you upset and angry. I hope that I have angered or upset you at least once by the end of this book. It is meant to convict you and cut you to the heart.

You are meant to think, "I know nothing."

Good. Then, God can teach you something. Blessed are the poor and the meek. Blessed are those that do not have and are hungry for they will be fed. A teacher makes you hungry so that God can feed you.

The evangelist prepares the ground. He digs that ground up and gets it going. Then, the teacher comes along with his seeds. Then, the pastor comes with his watering can, making sure that those seeds stay where they are meant to stay and flourish.

He makes sure that they get enough fertilizer and that they are taken care of day after day. I love how the fivefold ministry is such a team.

If you read through the entire series, you will see how all five of them work so beautifully together.

7. Trains You in Something New

The teacher also trains you in something new. I love the phrase, "training in righteousness". It does not say "understanding in righteousness".

When I hear the word "training", I am thinking "boot camp and weights". He trains you in righteousness. You receive an ability. You receive living knowledge.

You are either going to receive a principle or an anointing. You are going to receive something from the teacher that will train you. You will leave from them and live what they taught.

Circumstances will buffet you. Just like a weight trainer would take on weights to put pressure on his muscles, the teacher has this ability to release an anointing that causes those pressures to come on you so that you can be trained and equipped.

That is how he equips the Church. He releases that anointing through the Word. Circumstances are going to start happening in your life. You will say, "Lord, I cannot bear this weight. I cannot do it."

"Stand up. Learn to carry the weight. Push against it. When you learn to push against it with the principles that I have given you, you will rise up and grow. You will become trained, and you will be able to face the storms of life."

We need more teachers to release that anointing so that the Church starts living the gospel, instead of just sitting at church and understanding the gospel.

It is going to take a teacher with a teaching anointing to make them live it and not just understand it. In fact, I know that there are a lot of principles that you do not understand, and I am not stressed about that.

I do not need you to understand it. I just need you to receive it. The Holy Spirit is the one that teaches all things. You do not need any man to teach you. You do not need me to teach you.

You do not need a teacher to teach you - you need a teacher to release the anointing so that you can live it, and the Holy Spirit can teach you. That is our job.

8. Angered by Heresy

The teacher is angered by heresy. Do you want to see a teacher get upset? Have someone stand up in the church and sow some tares.

The teacher is convictional from the pulpit, but for the most part, we can be pretty even keel. Nothing really angers us, except when you are teaching heresy.

Do not stand up and talk a bunch of nonsense to the people that I love. Do not come and give them principles and Christian buzzwords that have no depth whatsoever, and have been spoken to death.

“Too blessed to be stressed?”

Seriously? That may not be heresy, but for the teacher, they are thinking, “Give me a break!”

Can we have just a little bit more depth to that? A teacher wants to see seeds out there. He wants to see reality, depth, and true meat. He does not want to hear the Christian blah blah that we hear all the time.

Now, the evangelists love those sayings and Christian buzzwords, and the prophets even like to jump in on them. However, the teacher is thinking, “You are so killing me. Really?”

Can we just kill the buzzwords? Between you and me, can we kill the “too blessed to be stressed” stuff? I do not want a t-shirt or a mug with that saying. Do not do that to me.

I will not appreciate it because teachers do not appreciate that kind of stuff. They would think, “Could we have not gotten a bit more original here?”

9. The Teacher Expresses the Nature of the Word to Us

The teacher expresses the nature of the Word to us. You can feel and taste the Lord in the Word. It is not just about knowledge. By the end of this chapter, you are not just taking away principles.

You are going to take away pictures and concepts. You are going to have a feeling in the pit of your stomach.

You are not going to understand this word right away. You are going to feel it.

It is shaping you. You feel it coming into you. You feel it going into your mind and spirit, and you are receiving a broad picture. That is the nature of the Word of God.

The nature of the Word is all encompassing. It is in you and out of you. It is a light and a lamp to your path and feet. It is also a bigger picture, a journey from beginning to end.

A teacher causes you to look back on your life and say, "I see the marker there and there." That is the nature of the Word of God.

When we read the Scriptures, we see the crucifixion in Genesis already. The Lord has a theme that He stitches through the eons, and it is so beautiful and poetic how it is all woven together. That is the nature of the Word.

It flows from one thing to the other. It flows from your ears, to your eyes, to your mind, to your heart, to your spirit, and then out through your actions.

The Word has so many characteristics. Sometimes, it is sharp, sometimes it is tender, sometimes it is a hammer on your head, and sometimes it is a foundation under your feet.

A teacher has the ability to bring that all together and bring your life together with it.

10. Flows in the Gifts – But DIFFERENTLY

He flows in the gifts of the spirit, but differently. Do you know that a teacher flows very well in visions? It is how they flow in visions that is a bit different. When they flow in visions, they see symbols of the Word.

For a prophet, it is different. They will see visions that are probably very strong to archetype, or something that the person can relate to. They may even use cartoon characters. It is going to be specific things that will help the person identify with their situation.

In fact, some of the visions that prophets get make you wonder if they even know the Word because it seems so outlandish.

However, the prophet is trying to draw that person into a relationship with Jesus, so they are going to share a vision that the person can relate to. It is going to touch on who that person is as a woman, a man, their archetype, or their work situation, and it is going to lead from there to a knowledge of Jesus.

This is not so for the teacher. When he gets a vision, it is going to be based on symbols in the Word. He is going to see a sword, a lamp, a river - something very specific and based on the Word.

Sometimes, since he has fed the Word into him, he will even see that scripture in a vision. It is just like Jesus saw when they were in the temple, and they were doing the ceremony of pouring water into the silver cup.

He said, "That is it people. That is what I have come to do. I have come to redeem your sin and wash you clean." That is how a teacher sees.

So, a teacher does flow in visions, and he can also flow in prophecy. Would it also interest you to know that teachers make the best dream interpreters?

The prophets may have the dream, but the teachers know how to interpret the dream better than anyone else I know. Why is that? It is because they know the language of the Word and the Spirit.

God speaks in the language of the Word to His prophets, and teachers get that because they are wired that way.

Can you not see that this is what the dream means? This is especially true when it is a prophetic dream, and the symbols in the dream are from Scriptures. Teachers just get that.

They flow very well in that, and they do not need to get revelation. They just know.

Yes, they flow in all of the gifts of the spirit actually. Just because you prophesy does not mean that you are a prophet. I am sure you are getting that.

> **The evangelist prophesies, the teacher prophesies, and the prophet prophesies. It is how they prophesy that differs. It is the anointing that they prophesy with that differs and how they view that revelation that differs.**

The teacher is going to see the symbols from the Word. As a teacher, you can ask God to flow that way. Perhaps, you did not think that you could, but you absolutely can.

In fact, when teachers flow that way, it tends to be quite solid because it is based on the Word, and they are not so swayed by the emotions that prophets are sometimes.

When you are prophetic, you can be a little emotional and get a few preconceived ideas in there. We can help you sort that out though by going through the training.

11. Ministry to the Church

Finally, the teacher is going to minister primarily to the Church. He is going to have a specific mandate. In the training, you will go through everything. It is a bit like a doctor.

Before they become specialists, they generally do training first. Every doctor studies the same first year of medical school. Then, they start to specialize. It is the same with the teacher.

You are going to go through all the problems, and you are going to experience everything. Then, further along in your training, God will start zeroing you to a specific avenue and mandate.

For some, you may be called to teach new believers. For others, you may be called to teach more mature believers. You may be called to teach the fivefold ministry or to teach on spiritual parenting.

You will start to see a progression in your ministry. That is what I love about the Lord. You cannot say, "This is it. I am going to be here for the rest of my life."

Maybe you are not like that, but I am not like that. I am grateful that the Lord allows places for people like us that can progress further and further in our calling, specializing more and more, and going deeper.

Above all, it is an anointing. We cannot do any of this without the Holy Spirit. You cannot get this kind of wisdom or revelation.

When the Lord started taking me through my teacher training, He made me work for it. I said, "Lord, I need this wisdom from the Word."

I had to bang on heaven's door. I had to beg, plead, fast, and pray. I had to seek Him. Yes, I could teach, but I did not want to just teach. I wanted the anointing. I wanted the teacher anointing.

I wanted people to live what I was teaching. I wanted it to be real. I did not want to sow tares. I sought Him and sought Him, and one day, I stood up and knew that what I was saying was God.

I knew that this was not my word, my Scripture, or my understanding. I was not teaching from the Word anymore. I was teaching as the Word. I stood there, and those visions flowed. Those scriptures flowed as visions.

Having gone through the prophetic, I understood what it was to flow in visions. This time, those scriptures flowed as visions. The character of the Word flowed as visions.

I did not have to understand or figure it out. I was my message. That is the day that I realized that God had made me into a teacher.

Press On!

I pray that we would have more that would go through the travail and pay the price. If you are at a place in your life where the Lord is making you seek, knock, and ask, do not give up.

Press through because there is something on the other side of that door for you. Maybe it does not come easy, but has it occurred to you that it is not meant to come easy?

God is not trying to withhold something from you. He wants to give you something that not many others have. It is the things that we travail long for that we love so much.

What mother after travailing for her newborn child does not absolutely fall head over heels the moment that they are born?

The things that we work the hardest for are the things that we love the most.

When you work for the Word and for that anointing, when you invest all you are and give up all that you are to take hold of His nature and character and revel in it, you are going to become the kind of teacher that will lay a doctrinal foundation for this Church.

Then, we are going to see a move of God, an apostolic move of God, take place. So, put your sword in your hand and stop messing around. Teachers, the Church needs you.

About the Author

Born in Bulawayo, Zimbabwe and raised in South Africa, Colette had a zeal to serve the Lord from a young age. Coming from a long line of Christian leaders and having grown up as a pastor's kid, she is no stranger to the realities of ministry. Despite having to endure many hardships such as her parent's divorce, rejection, and poverty, she continues to follow after the Lord passionately. Overcoming these obstacles early in her life has built a foundation of compassion and desire to help others gain victory in their lives.

Since then, the Lord has led Colette, with her husband, Craig Toach, to establish *Apostolic Movement International,* a ministry to train and minister to Christian leaders all over the world, where they share all the wisdom that the Lord has given them through each and every time they chose to walk through the refining fire in their personal lives, as well as in ministry.

In addition, Colette is a fantastic cook, an amazing mom to not only her 4 natural children, but to her numerous spiritual children all over the world. Colette is also a renowned author, mentor, trainer and a woman that has great taste in shoes! The scripture to "be all things to all men" definitely applies here, and the Lord keeps adding to that list of things each and every day.

How does she do it all? Experience through every book and teaching the life of an apostle firsthand, and get the insight into how the call of God can make every aspect of your life an incredible adventure.

Read more at www.colette-toach.com

Connect with Colette Toach on Facebook!
www.facebook.com/ColetteToach

Check Colette out on Amazon.com at:
www.amazon.com/author/colettetoach

Recommendations by the Author

Note: All reference of AMI refers to Apostolic Movement International.

If you enjoyed this book, I know you will also love the following books and recommendations.

The Fivefold Offices for Today

Book 1 of the Fivefold Office Series

By Colette Toach

The fivefold ministry has been a mystery that is only being resurrected in the Church today.

You see people rising up with the different callings, you see how God brings these different individuals together, and calls them to set the Church afire, but what are the fivefold offices exactly, and where do you fit in?

Are you an Apostle, Prophet, Teacher, Pastor, or Evangelist? Are you called to walk the social, business, or ministry road? It is time to reveal the road ahead of you, and to rise up into the fullness of your call.

Where you are now is great, but God has so much more in store for you than you realize. It is time to take hold of the reality of your call to the fivefold offices.

Today's Evangelist

Book 2 of the Fivefold Office Series

By Colette Toach

As an evangelist, you are called to start churches, to bring life to the dead, to bring people into the embrace of the Holy Spirit, and open their eyes to the power of Christ.

In this book, Colette will show you where the evangelist came from, what their role is in the fivefold ministry, and how and where they operate. So be prepared to go higher and understand your call as an evangelist like never before.

Today's Pastor

Book 3 of the Fivefold Office Series

By Colette Toach

In this book, Colette takes you on a journey through your life and paints a picture of what today's pastor really looks like, and supposed to be doing.

Perhaps you have felt that pull already, the pull of those sheep coming to you for help, and sharing things they really shouldn't, because they feel you will be able to help them. Welcome to being a pastor! It is time to discover what that truly means.

The Minister's Handbook

By Colette Toach

This is your manual on effective ministry. Whether you are dealing with an unexpected demon manifestation or you need to give marital counsel, you will find the answers here.

Colette Toach gives it to you in plain language. She gives you the steps 1, 2, 3 of how to do what God has called you to do. Keep a copy on hand, because you will come back to it time and time again!

How to Hear the Voice of God (Study Group Kit)

By Colette Toach

Knowing the Lord is more than just understanding the principles of the Word. It is learning to know when He is speaking and to share in the secrets in His heart.

By the time you are finished with this course, you will discover that God does not have favorites, but that every believer can hear from Him clearly.

If you are ready to experience the reality of the Lord in your life, then dive in!

Fivefold Ministry School

www.fivefold-school.com

You Can Be a Success in Ministry!

My passion is to see you realize yours! I understand the years in the desert. I know what it feels like to have a fire shut up in your bones, knowing that God has something greater for you.

That is why together with my husband Craig Toach, we have trained up our own Fivefold Ministry team and in association with apostles all over the world, we hold in our hands the resources to launch you into your ministry!

Here is What We Offer to Prepare You for Your Fivefold Ministry Calling

- Identify Your Fivefold Ministry Calling
- Disciple and Mentor Relationship
- Ministry Certification, Credentials and Ordination
- Ministry Training Materials That Are Totally Unique
- Fivefold Ministry Training That Affects More Than Your Mind
- Student Only Benefits

Contact Information

To check out our wide selection of materials, go to:
www.ami-bookshop.com

Do you have any questions about any products?

Contact us at: +1 (760) 466 - 7679
(9am to 5pm California Time, Weekdays Only)

E-mail Address: admin@ami-bookshop.com

Postal Address:

A.M.I.
5663 Balboa Ave #416
San Diego, CA 92111, USA

Facebook Page:
http://www.facebook.com/ApostolicMovementInternational

YouTube Page:
https://www.youtube.com/c/ApostolicMovementInternational

Twitter Page: https://twitter.com/apmoveint

Amazon.com Page: www.amazon.com/author/colettetoach

AMI Bookshop – It's not Just Knowledge, It's **Living Knowledge**

Made in the USA
Middletown, DE
21 October 2023

41210765R00070